Looking
will see that many of the things you take for granted ...
life are based on what we call "human rights". These rights
include the right to live freely, say what you think, and be
treated fairly and with dignity by others.

These rights are the rights of every human being, and they are
guaranteed by a number of texts, including the Council of
Europe's Human Rights Convention. They have not always
existed, however. In fact, winning them has taken centuries, and
we owe them to the many brave women and men who have
fought to make them a reality, often at the cost of their own
lives. Even today, the struggle has to go on, for there are still
men, women and children to whom they are denied.

These pages will show you that the law is there to protect your
life and freedom, to allow you to speak your mind without fear
of the consequences. To make the society you live in as just and
fair as it can be, it is important for you to know what your rights
are, and also that your rights are protected.

The main purpose of "human rights" is to protect the weak, the
vulnerable, the people who cannot always protect themselves.
You must never forget that the rights explained in this book are
the rights of all men and women, and that living as part of the
human community means that your rights must take into
account other people's rights, that your freedom stops where
other people's freedom begins.

When you finish this book, you will remember that the Council
of Europe's Human Rights Convention is not something fixed
and final, but something which evolves and develops as daily life
goes on. Rights themselves have evolved in the course of
human history. They are still evolving today and they are, in the
form in which we know them, a precious but fragile heritage. It
will be up to you to take care of it, breathe life into it and make
it grow.

C. Lalumière

Catherine Lalumière
Secretary General of the Council of Europe

The Council of Europe

has 27 member countries at present. You can find a list of them at the end of this Album. The Council's headquarters are in Strasbourg.

The Council of Europe's flag is the European flag.
It consists of a circle of 12 gold stars on a blue ground.
The arrangement of the stars in a circle symbolises union.
The figure 12, is a symbol of perfection and completeness.

One of the Council of Europe's aims is to protect and develop Human Rights and Democracy a little better each day in the interest of greater justice, equality and dignity for all men, women and children.

The Council of Europe also deals with all questions affecting Society, with the exception of defence problems.

There are several other European organisations you often hear about, such as: The EC or European Community. At present it has 12 members: Belgium, Denmark, France, Germany, Greece, Ireland, Italy, Luxembourg, the Netherlands, Portugal, Spain and the United Kingdom.
Its various institutions include the European Council (consisting of the Heads of State or Government of the 12 EC countries) and the European Parliament (whose members are elected by direct suffrage in the EC countries).

Here are the meanings of some of the complicated words you will find when reading this Album:

Convention:
an agreement or contract to be observed by every country which signs it.

Ratification:
confirmation by a Country's Parliament of the commitment it accepted when signing a convention.

Protocol:
a legal text added later to a convention.

Democracy:
a country where people are free and equal, where their rights are protected by the law and justice and where they can choose the individuals who govern them.

Dictatorship:
the opposite of democracy.

Oppression:
the absence of freedom.

Intolerance:
not accepting that other people think or act differently.

Xenophobia:
being hostile to foreign people or things.

Racism:
thinking that some races are superior to others and acting accordingly.

Ultranationalism:
excessive dedication to one's own country, without any respect for the values which bring all human beings together.

Rule of law:
a situation where citizens' rights are protected by the law and where the enforcement of the law is ensured by an independent judicial system.

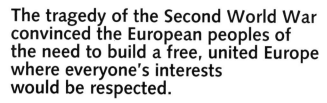

The tragedy of the Second World War convinced the European peoples of the need to build a free, united Europe where everyone's interests would be respected.

It was for that reason that the **Council of Europe was founded in 1949 as a bulwark against oppression and the dangers of dictatorship...**

In order to become members of the Council of Europe, States must promise to respect **Democracy, Human Rights and the Rule of Law**.

These values are the basic principles of a fairer society. But they can never be taken for granted, for unfortunately, they are sometimes put at risk, even nowadays, by such things as intolerance, racism, xenophobia, and ultranationalism. They must therefore be protected with a great deal of vigilance.

In order to protect them, the Council of Europe drew up the **European Convention on Human Rights**.
This Convention does more than simply proclaim a series of rights and freedoms for everybody living in the member States; it makes sure they are enforced by a European Court and Commission of Human Rights which you can about read on pages 28 and 29.

This means that any man, woman or child who considers that his or her Convention-based rights have been violated **can lodge a complaint against whichever Government is considered responsible**.

Later, the Council of Europe supplemented the European Convention on Human Rights with other texts, such as the European Social Charter and the European Convention for the Prevention of Torture and Inhuman or Degrading Treatment or Punishment.

When reading this Album, you will also see that the Council of Europe - a sort of great observatory monitoring what goes on throughout Europe, in the East, the West, the North and the South - is implementing a whole range of measures to prevent situations from arising where Human Rights could be flouted.

Protecting Human Rights and doing everything to ensure that they are respected is the most effective way to preserve peace. This is the responsibility of everyone - including you.

Everyone's right to life shall be pr
(Article 2)

We shall be looking at 21 articles of the European Convention on Human Rights and its Protocols, as well as 11 illustrations. The Convention is based on the Universal Declaration of Human Rights, the first article of which reads:
"All human beings are born free and equal in dignity and rights."

ted by law.

Abolition of the death penalty.
(Protocol No. 6 - Article 1)

Even though more and more States have abolished the death penalty, this Protocol, dating from 1983, has still not been ratified by all countries...
What is the situation in your country?

It is important to know that a State which has ratified the European Convention on Human Rights is obliged to observe articles of the actual Convention but can choose whether to accept the Protocols to the Convention.

No one shall be subjected to torture or torture or inhuman or degrading treatment or punishment.

(Article 3)

There are many different forms of torture and inhuman or degrading treatment or punishment.

In order to **help States** to apply Article 3, the Council of Europe drew up the "Convention for the Prevention of Torture and Inhuman or Degrading Treatment or Punishment".

The main purpose of this Convention is a **preventive** one. It is designed to help States to do all they can to ensure that people deprived of their liberty are protected and prevent situations from arising that might lead to torture.

For that reason a **committee** has been set up to visit places of detention of any kind: prisons, police stations, military barracks, psychiatric hospitals, etc.

No one shall be held in slavery or servitude.

(Article 4)

Right to liberty and security.
(Article 5)

No one may be deprived of liberty unless lawfully detained.

Everyone charged with a criminal offence shall be presumed innocent until proved guilty according to law.
(Article 6.2)

Right to a fair trial

(Article 6)
We all have the right to be heard and tried by an independent and impartial tribunal within a reasonable time.

11

Everyone has the right to respect
and family life, his home and his
(Article 8)

The right of men
and women
to marry and
found a family
(Article 12)

The righ

his private
espondence.

the peaceful enjoyment of possessions
(First Protocol - Article 1)

No person shall be denied the right to education.

(First Protocol - Article 2)

This right belongs to us all whoever we are, whatever our national or social origins may be, whether we are male or female...

This article also specifies that, in carrying out its educational functions, a State must respect the right of parents to provide their children with an education in keeping with their own religious or philosophical convictions. Of course, nothing in that education should conflict with the rights of the children themselves.

Equality of both parents' rights in respect of their children.

(Protocol 7 - Article 5).

Freedom of thought, conscience an

(Article 9)

eligion.

This right includes freedom to change one's religion or belief as well as freedom to manifest one's religion or belief, both alone and in a group, in public and in private, whether one is, for example, Agnostic, Atheistic, Catholic, Jewish, Moslem, Orthodox or Protestant - while respecting everybody else's rights.

Freedom of expression. Freedom of opinion
Freedom to receive or communicate inform
(Article 10)

on or ideas.

Any form of communication - self-expression, voicing of opinions, imparting of information - involves everyone's responsibility - yours and mine, the responsibility of others and that of the media. When expressing ourselves, we should bear this in mind and respect the dignity and liberty of others.

Obligation for member States to hold free elections by secret ballot in order to choose the members of the legislature.
(First Protocol - Article 3)

Freedom of peaceful assembly and freedom of association. Right to form and join trade unions for the protection of one's interests.
(Article 11)

It is intolerable not only to be deprived of liberty but also to live in absolute destitution. What is the good of having your right to life protected by law (Article 2) if you are starving to death?

For that reason it is just as important to protect social and economic rights - which is what the Council of Europe tries to do through the European Social Charter.

This Charter calls on member States to guarantee 23 social and economic rights covering such matters as working conditions, a fair wage, the right to strike and the protection of children and women at work.

You see, these rights are also human rights.

Freedom of movement. Freedom to leav

(Protocol No. 4 - Article 2)

No one shall be
expelled from the
territory of the State
of which he or she is
a national or be
deprived of the right
to enter his or her
own country.
(Protocol 4 - Article 3)

C

ny country, including one's own.

ective expulsion of aliens is prohibited.
(Protocol 4 -Article 4)

These rights and freedoms must be secure
on any ground such as sex, race, colour, la
other opinion, national or social origin, ass
minority, property, birth or other status...

(Article 14)

You have not only rights
but also responsibilities.
This means that nothing
in the Convention may
be interpreted as
entitling you to do
something that might
interfere with the rights
and freedoms protected
by the Convention.

(Article 17)

without discrimination uage, religion, political or ation with a national

To ensure observance of the Co
Human Rights and a European

(Article 19)

The European Commission of Human Rights and the European Court of Human Rights are both judicial bodies. In other words, they are a kind of court. Their members are elected, and they act completely independently of the member States.

ention, a European Commission of
urt of Human Rights have been set up.

The protective machinery of the European Convention on Human Rights

The **European Commission of Human Rights** (set up in 1954) holds sessions in private to examine complaints lodged against States accused of failing to respect the rights and freedoms set out in the European Convention on Human Rights.

Complaints may be lodged against a State by an individual, a group of individuals (organisation, association, etc.) or another State.

For a complaint to be declared admissible by the Commission, the person lodging it must demonstrate that every possible form of legal action in the country concerned has been attempted.

If a complaint is declared admissible, the Commission will first of all try to settle the matter on a friendly basis. If this attempt fails, it will issue an impartial and objective opinion on the case.

The **European Court of Human Rights** (set up in 1959) consists of judges equal in number to the number of member States (one per State).
The Court examines cases referred to it by the European Commission of Human Rights or the state concerned.
It summons to a public hearing the two parties' lawyers and the delegate(s) of the Commission.
After the hearing, the judges deliberate in private and deliver their judgment. Their judgments are reached by a majority vote.

The **Committee of Ministers** is the decision-making body of the Council of Europe. It is made up of the Foreign Affairs Ministers of the member States or their Deputies.
The Committee decides on certain cases not referred to the Court and is responsible for supervising the execution of the Court's judgments.

I would like to receive more
information * about :

Name

Address

* in English   in French
* delete as necessary

Council of Europe
Palais de l'Europe
Point info
B.P. 431 R6
F-67006 Strasbourg

Council of Europe Press
ISBN 92-871-2095-1
© Council of Europe, 1992
Printed in Belgium

Polish edition :
Album Praw Człowieka
ISBN 92-871-2096-X

French edition :
L'album des droits de l'homme
ISBN 92-871-2094-3

Do you want to know more about the Council of Europe?

If you want some further information about:

- The European Convention on Human Rights
- The European Social Charter
- The European Convention for the Prevention of Torture and Inhuman or Degrading Treatment or Punishment
- The protection of Human Rights in Europe
- The European Court of Human Rights
- The European Commission of Human Rights
- Work on equality between women and men
- or any other subject

Send this card, for an answer, to:
Council of Europe
Point info
B.P. 431 R6
67006 Strasbourg
FRANCE

The Council of Europe is also:

The **Committee of Ministers**, made up of the Foreign Affairs Ministers of the member countries, which takes the political decisions.

The **Parliamentary Assembly**, comprising parliamentarians who are also members of the member countries' Parliaments, which debates major current issues and makes recommendations to the Committee of Ministers.

The **Standing Conference of Local and Regional Authorities**, which consists of mayors and elected regional representatives of member countries.

The European Youth Centre.

A set of 140 international Agreements or Conventions on such subjects as

the rights of foreigners and migrant workers (workers from less developed regions who go abroad in search of work),
a European Code of Social Security guaranteeing a minimum level of social protection,
transfrontier television, the aim being to foster pluralism, diversity and choice,
the protection of natural habitats and the improvement of the environment
violence at sports events, etc...

Studies and proposals on :

education and cultural life in Europe,
medical research and the use of embryos and foetuses,
combating AIDS and drug addiction,
protecting children from ill-treatment,
preventing violence in families ("battered wives" problem),
equality between women and men, etc...

This is a whole panoply of awareness-raising measures, ideas, data, contacts, guidelines or obligations aimed at eliminating arbitrary decisions and powers as far as possible and promoting European co-operation for the sake of mutual recognition and respect.

The European Court of Human Rights has already dealt with cases concerning such questions as:

- detention
- the length of judicial proceedings
- telephone tapping
- social security
- compulsory sex education in schools
- corporal punishment in schools
- the status of illegitimate children
- parents' access to children in public care
- property
- trade-union activities
- freedom of expression
- immigration
- extradition
- etc…